WEIGHT

Chris Woodford

Gareth Stevens
Publishing

Please visit our website, www.garethstevens.com. For a free color catalog of all our high-quality books, call toll-free 1-800-542-2595 or fax 1-877-542-2596.

Library of Congress Cataloging-in-Publication Data

Woodford, Chris.
Weight / Chris Woodford.
    p. cm. — (Measure up math)
Includes index.
ISBN 978-1-4339-7462-5 (pbk.)
ISBN 978-1-4339-7463-2 (6-pack)
ISBN 978-1-4339-7461-8 (library binding)
1. Weights and measures—Juvenile literature. I. Title.
QC106.W659 2013
530.8'1—dc23
                                2011045524

Published in 2013 by
Gareth Stevens Publishing
111 East 14th Street, Suite 349
New York, NY 10003

© 2013 Brown Bear Books Ltd

For Brown Bear Books Ltd:
Editorial Director: Lindsey Lowe
Managing Editor: Tim Harris
Children's Publisher: Anne O'Daly
Art Director: Jeni Child
Designer: Lynne Lennon
Picture Manager: Sophie Mortimer
Production Director: Alastair Gourlay

Picture Credits:
Key: t = top, tl = top left, b = bottom
Front Cover: istockphoto
Interior: NASA: 5; Shutterstock: Semjonow Juri 25, Lagui 14, Sevenke 29b, Feng Yu 20, Zurijea 4; SuperStock: Imagebroker 16; Thinkstock: BananaStock 22, Comstock 24–25 Dreatas 26–27, Hemera 12–13t, istock 19tl, PhotoObjects 8, Stockbyte 10. All other artworks and photographs Brown Bear Books Ltd.
Brown Bear Books has made every attempt to contact the copyright holder. If anyone has any information could they please contact smortimer@windmillbooks.co.uk

All Artworks © Brown Bear Books Ltd

Publisher's note to educators and parents: Our editors have carefully reviewed the websites that appear on p. 31 to ensure that they are suitable for students. Many websites change frequently, however, and we cannot guarantee that a site's future contents will continue to meet our high standards of quality and educational value. Be advised that students should be closely supervised whenever they access the Internet.

Manufactured in the United States of America
1 2 3 4 5 6 7 8 9   12 11 10

CPSIA compliance information: Batch #BRS12GS: For further information contact Gareth Stevens, New York, New York at 1-800-542-2595.

CONTENTS

WHAT IS WEIGHT?

▶▶▶ **H**ave you ever tried to pick up something very heavy and not been able to? Heavy things have lots of weight. Their weight is caused by gravity. Gravity is a force that pulls things toward Earth. Heavy things are pulled toward Earth more than light things.

Mass and weight

Things have weight because they have mass, but mass and weight are different. Mass is the amount of matter something is made from. Matter is anything that takes up space and has weight. Solids, such as metals, plastics, and wood, are examples of matter. Liquids (such as water) and gases (such as air) are matter, too.

▶ **The mass of this girl's books will always be the same. But their weight would change if she took them up a mountain.**

A truck has more mass than a car because it contains more metal. Because a truck has more mass, gravity pulls it toward Earth more. That is why a truck weighs more than a car.

Gravity changes

Gravity is stronger or weaker at different places on Earth. Suppose a person drove a car up a mountain. At the top of the mountain, the car would weigh a little less than it did at the bottom. That is because gravity is weaker at the top of a mountain than at the bottom. But its mass would stay the same—mass never changes.

FACT

If a girl travels from New York to Denver, she will get slightly lighter. Gravity is a tiny bit less there.

WORD BANK   *Gravity: the force that pulls things toward Earth*

5

WEIGHT THROUGH THE AGES

▶▶▶ **P**eople have been weighing things for thousands of years. We know this because some people dig up places to find evidence of how others lived many years ago. They have found weights buried in 6,000-year-old graves in Egypt.

▼ **Two thousand years ago, the Romans needed to know the weight of the stone blocks they used in their building projects.**

Animal-shaped weights

Many ancient Egyptian weights have been found. Some of these weights are just lumps of stone. Others have been carved into shapes like animals, including birds, beetles, and even people.

Two thousand years ago, the ancient Romans invented the weights we now use—the ounce, pound, and ton. The Roman word for pound was *libra*. That is why the abbreviation for pound is *lb*. Around 1800, the French people became the first to use the metric system for measuring things. Many other countries, but not the United States, have switched to the metric system since then.

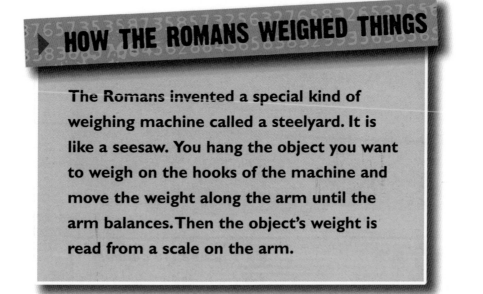

▶ HOW THE ROMANS WEIGHED THINGS

The Romans invented a special kind of weighing machine called a steelyard. It is like a seesaw. You hang the object you want to weigh on the hooks of the machine and move the weight along the arm until the arm balances. Then the object's weight is read from a scale on the arm.

WORD BANK *Ounce: a small weight; there are 16 ounces in a pound*

OUNCES AND POUNDS

Most likely, you know your weight in pounds. Pounds are called imperial measures. A pound is a fairly small weight. An ordinary-sized bag of table sugar weighs five pounds. People can measure lighter things in ounces. There are 16 ounces in a pound. Two pencils weigh about 1 ounce.

◀ These metal weights are used to weigh things on scales. People use a small weight to weigh something small and a larger weight to weigh something bigger.

1 *1 ounce*
2 *2 ounces*
3 *4 ounces*
4 *8 ounces (¹/₂ pound)*
5 *1 pound (16 ounces)*
6 *2 pounds*
7 *3 pounds*

Bigger weights

People need bigger units to weigh heavier things. Heavy things like sacks of coal are sometimes measured in hundredweights. A hundredweight is the same as 100 pounds. A big sack of flour weighs about a hundredweight.

People can measure even heavier things, like cars and trucks, using tons. A ton is sometimes called a short ton and is the same as 2,000 pounds. A small car weighs about a ton.

Pounds, hundredweight, and tons are units of weight. A unit is something that says how big a measurement is. Three pounds is a smaller weight than three hundredweight. Three tons is heavier than three hundredweight. In these examples, the number three means something different each time. The unit tells us what it means.

FACT

A loaf of bread weighs about 1 pound (16 ounces). So does a small melon.

▶ **TRY THIS**

HOW MUCH DOES THAT WEIGH?
Use scales or ask a grown-up to find the missing weights.

Pencil	*? ounces*
Bag of table sugar	*5 pounds*
Bag of flour	*? pounds*
Baby	*8 pounds*
Boy (aged 10)	*? pounds*
Woman	*140 pounds*
Man	*? pounds*
Large car	*2 tons*
Truck	*? tons*
Earth	*600,000,000,000,000,000,000 tons = 600 quintillion tons*

Answers on page 31.

WORD BANK   *Pound: a unit of weight that equals 16 ounces*

WEIGHING IN METRIC

Outside the United States, many people use a set of measures called the metric system. The metric system of weights is based around the kilogram. One kilogram weighs about as much as a big can of tomatoes. That is about the same as 2.2 pounds. So if a person weighs 180 pounds, we could

▲ This 10-year-old boy weighs 70 pounds. This is the same as 32 kilograms using a metric unit of weight.

also say that they weigh 81 kilograms (kg).
That is because 180 divided by 2.2 is 81.

There are bigger and smaller measures than
kilograms in the metric system. The smallest
metric weight most people use is the gram.
An ounce is the same as 28 grams, so a gram
is a very small weight.

▶ **TRY THIS**   + – = x + – = x + – = x +

CHANGING TO AND FROM METRIC

Imperial to metric
- 1 ounce is the same as 28 grams
  How many grams are there in 3 ounces?
- 16 ounces, or 1 pound, is the same as 454
  grams, or 0.45 kilogram
  How many grams are there in 5 pounds?
- 1 short ton is the same as 0.9 metric ton

Metric to imperial
- 1 gram is the same as 0.04 ounce
  How many ounces are there in 6 grams?
- 1 kilogram is the same as 2.2 pounds
  How many pounds are there in 10 kilograms?
- 1 metric ton is the same as 1.1 short tons

Answers on page 31.

+ – = x + – = x + – = x + – = x + – = – =

WORD BANK   *Kilogram: a metric unit of weight equal to 1,000 grams*

WEIGHING WITH SCALES

▶▶▶ **C**hildren can compare their weights by sitting on a seesaw. Suppose two friends sit on either end of the seesaw at the same distance from the middle. When they lift up their legs, if one end of the seesaw goes down farther than the other, then the child on that end weighs more.

Balancing weights

Lots of weighing machines work like seesaws. These machines are called scales or balances. They have two pans, one on either side. They also have a set of weights of different sizes. The weights can be lifted on and off the pans. To weigh an object, you put it on one pan. Then you put weights on the other pan. When the scales balance, there is the same weight on each side. If you count the weights, you know how much the object weighs.

You can also put the weights on first. To measure 10 ounces of candies, for example, a shopkeeper puts 10 ounces of weights on one pan. Then she or he pours candies into the other pan until the scales balance.

FACT

The Ashrita seesaw in St. Louis is the world's largest. It is 79 feet (24 meters) long.

COUNTING BY WEIGHING

In a bank, you will see that the tellers do not count coins. Instead, they weigh them. Each coin weighs the same. By weighing the coins, the teller can figure out how many coins there are.

> 1 quarter weighs 0.2 ounce
>
> 1 nickel weighs 5 grams

If a bag of quarters weighs 12 ounces, how many quarters are there?

If a pile of nickels weighs 100 grams, how many nickels are there?

Answers on page 31.

+ − = x + − = x + − = x + − = x + −

◀ Seesaws are a bit like balancing scales. The boy who is raised above the ground weighs less than his friend.

WORD BANK *Scales: a weighing machine, often with two pans*

OTHER WAYS TO WEIGH

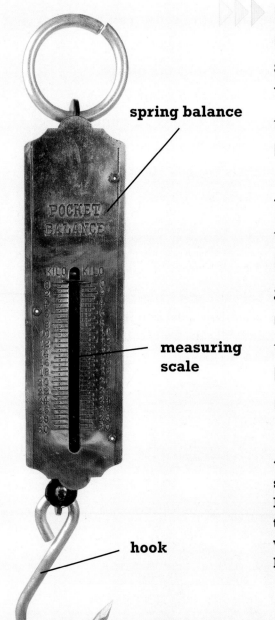

spring balance

POCKET BALANCE

KILO KILO

measuring scale

hook

Not all scales and balances have two pans. Some have a single pan on top and, beneath the pan, a dial with a pointer. The dial may be round, with the scale around the outside. Or it may be long and thin like a ruler.

To use a weighing device like this, you first set the pointer so it lines up with the zero mark. Next, you put something on the pan. The pan goes down and the pointer turns around or moves from left to right on the scale. You then read the weight on the dial. The dial has a scale on it marked in imperial or metric units, or both.

◀ This is a kind of spring balance. It works only if the item to be weighed can be hung on the hook.

FACT

When it has a full load, the heaviest dump truck ever made weighs 758 tons (688 metric tons).

Spring balances

Scales like this are sometimes called spring balances because they have a spring inside. When you put a weight on the pan, it pushes downward. That squashes the spring inside.

The heavier the weight, the more the spring squashes. As the spring squashes, it moves the pointer around the dial or along the scale. When the weight is taken off again, the spring goes back to its old shape.

▼ **When the cherries were added to the pan, the pointer on the dial moved from left to right. The pointer shows the weight of the cherries.**

pan

scale

pointer

WORD BANK *Weighbridge: a huge balance used for weighing trucks and cars*

SMALL WEIGHTS

Light things have weight, just as heavy things do. A piece of paper does not weigh very much, but it still has weight. Even the air around us has weight. Earth's gravity pulls air toward it. That makes the cloud of gases called the atmosphere. Without the atmosphere, people could not breathe and plants could not grow. Light things do not weigh much, but sometimes people still need to weigh them.

Accurate scales

People need very accurate scales and balances to weigh

troy weight

▶ **Jewelers use tiny scales and troy weights like these to measure small jewels.**

very light things. They cannot use units like pounds and tons. They have to use smaller units instead. Jewelers, for example, use a measuring system called troy weights. In the troy system, there are units of weight called ounces, pennyweights, and grains. There are 24 grains in a pennyweight. Twenty pennyweights make 1 troy ounce, and 12 troy ounces make 1 troy pound. Four troy pounds make 1 imperial pound.

Carats

A carat is a very light measurement of weight. One carat is the same as 200 milligrams, or 0.2 gram. Diamonds are usually weighed in carats. A diamond that weighs 1 carat is about ¼ inch (6 millimeters) in diameter.

▼ **A housefly is very light. It weighs about 12 milligrams in the metric system. That is less than ¼ grain in the troy system.**

▶ **MILLIGRAMS**

In the metric system, people weigh light things using milligrams (mg). There are 1,000 milligrams in a gram, so a milligram is a very light weight. A housefly's wing weighs about 1 milligram.

WORD BANK *Gram: a small unit of weight in the metric system*

DENSITY AND WEIGHT

▶▶▶ **U**sually, bigger things weigh more than smaller ones. So, a boulder weighs more than a pebble. But that is not always true. If you have ever picked up a large gold coin, you will know that it is much heavier than it looks. So we cannot always tell how much something weighs just by looking at it.

Suppose we have a block of wood and a lump of metal that are exactly the same size. The metal weighs more than the wood because metal is more dense than wood. Density is a measure of how much matter something contains.

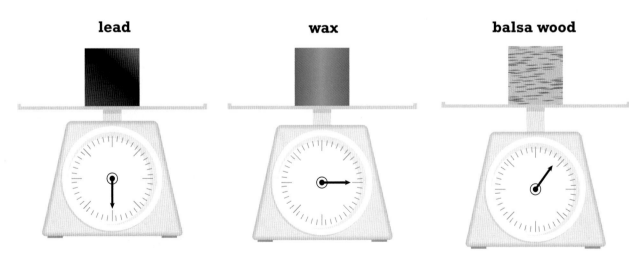

lead **wax** **balsa wood**

▲ **Blocks of lead, wax, and balsa wood of the same size have different weights. The lead is the heaviest. The balsa wood is the lightest.**

Everything on Earth has density. Density means how dense something is, or how closely its atoms are packed together. Usually solids are more dense than liquids, and liquids are more dense than gases. Gold is one of the densest solids on Earth. Bars of gold like these are very heavy indeed.

Invisible particles

Everything is made of matter, and all matter is made up of tiny invisible particles called atoms. The atoms that make up a piece of metal are heavier and closer together than those in wood. So a piece of metal weighs more than a piece of wood of the same size.

FACT

A block of wood with a volume of 120 cubic feet will weigh the same as 1 cubic foot of gold.

WORD BANK   *Atom: a tiny particle; all matter is made up of atoms*

THINGS THAT FLOAT

▲ These logs weigh a lot, but they still float on water. This is because they are less dense than the water.

Some things float on water while others do not. Wooden things are good at floating. Even huge logs will float. Metal things tend to sink. Even a paper clip will sink in water. Density is what makes one thing float and something else sink. Wood is less dense than water, so wood floats. Metal is more dense than water. That is why metal sinks.

Making heavy things float

Sometimes heavy things can be made to float. A block of metal normally sinks. But if the block of metal is made into a large hollow box—for example, a boat—it will float. On average, the materials the box is made of—including the air inside it—are less dense than the water it is floating on. That is why boats and ships float on water.

FACT

When full of oil, the supertanker Mont weighed 724,000 tons but still stayed afloat!

▶ HOW LOW CAN IT GO?

An oil-tanker ship is a little like an empty metal box. It takes up a certain space, or volume. When the ship is loaded with oil, it is much heavier. The volume of the ship does not change, but its mass becomes greater. So, the more oil the tanker carries, the denser it is and the lower it floats in the water. If the tanker's density is less than the density of water, the tanker floats. If its density is more than the density of water, the tanker sinks.

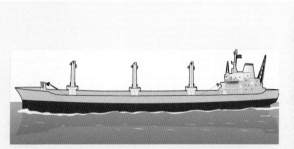

▲ An empty oil tanker is like an empty metal box. It floats on the sea because its density is less than that of water.

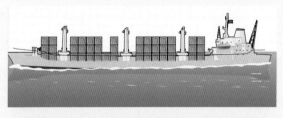

▲ When it is full of oil, the tanker floats much lower in the water because it is much denser and weighs more.

WORD BANK   *Density: a measure of how much matter something contains*

USEFUL WEIGHTS

People need to weigh things for many reasons. One reason is so they know how much of something they are buying. Many foods are sold by weight. People pay a certain amount of money for a certain weight of food. Weights also come in handy in cooking. Recipes tell us how to cook things. A recipe is a list of ingredients. It tells us how much of each ingredient we have to use.

▲ When buying the ingredients for baking or cooking, it is important to get the right weight of each one.

Ingredients and recipes

Sometimes recipes ask you to measure ingredients by volume, using measurements like cups or teaspoons. At other times, people have to weigh the ingredients using scales. If we use too much or too little of something, the recipe may turn out wrong.

Weights are also important in chemistry. Chemistry is the study of materials. Many of the materials we use are made by adding two or more substances together. We have to weigh chemicals before we can join them to create new chemicals.

CHEMICAL WEIGHTS

In chemistry, there are more than 100 different substances called elements. Every substance on Earth is made of very tiny particles called atoms. Atoms weigh very little, and chemists have special ways to weigh them. Each element is made of a different type of atom. For example, hydrogen is made of hydrogen atoms, and gold is made of gold atoms. Hydrogen (a gas) is the lightest element known. The heaviest element that exists in nature is a metal called uranium. Uranium atoms weigh much more than hydrogen atoms.

WORD BANK   *Gas: a substance, such as air, that spreads to fill space*

BODY WEIGHTS

▶▶▶ **D**octors weigh newborn babies regularly to see if they are growing properly. As people get older, they get bigger, taller, and heavier. People often weigh themselves by standing on scales to see how heavy they are.

If you are a certain height and age, you should weigh a certain amount. If you weigh much more than this, you may be overweight. If you weigh

▶ **TRY THIS**

+ – = x + – = x + – = x + – =

HOW MUCH DO ANIMALS WEIGH COMPARED TO HUMANS ?

Work out the missing weights (pounds or kilograms) where there is a question mark.

Earthworm	*5 ounces, or ? grams*
Cat	*8 pounds, or 3.6 kilograms*
Dog	*? pounds, or 36 kilograms*
Adult human	*160 pounds, or ? kilograms*
Panda	*? pounds, or 136 kilograms*
Elephant	*7 tons, or 6.3 metric tons*

Answers on page 31.

+ – = x + – = x + – = x + – = x + – = + – =

much less, you may be underweight. Usually people are healthier if they are not overweight or underweight. If you eat well and do lots of exercise, your weight is probably just right.

Healthy weights

Doctors can sometimes tell if people are healthy or unwell by weighing them. If people have lost a lot of weight, that might mean they are sick. If people have been sick and they start to put weight back on, it might mean that they are getting better again. So doctors find weighing people is very helpful.

▼ A fully grown African elephant weighs 7 tons. That is about the same as 180 11-year-old children.

INCREDIBLE WEIGHTS

People cannot see gravity, so they cannot really see weight. But sometimes very heavy things, such as heavy birds, are hard to miss. The heaviest bird that flies is the mute swan. It weighs up to 50 pounds (22.5 kilograms) but can still use its huge wings to get off the ground. About 1,000 years ago a bird called the elephant bird weighed as much as seven men!

▶ TRY THIS

WEIGHING VEGETABLES AND FRUIT

Ask an adult's permission to use the kitchen scales, then weigh any vegetables or fruit you have at home. Here are some examples: apples, bananas, carrots, melons, onions, oranges, pears, and potatoes. Write down your answers in imperial and metric units. List them with the heaviest first and the lightest last.

► MONSTER VEGETABLES

It is not just animals that can grow to amazing weights. Around the world, people hold competitions to see how big they can grow vegetables and fruit. In 2010, someone grew a pumpkin that weighed 1,810 pounds (821 kilograms). These monster foods look amazing, but often they do not taste very good.

Weight lifters

Some creatures can carry huge weights. An elephant can carry a quarter of its own weight on its back, around 1¾ tons, or 1.6 metric tons. A leaf-cutter ant can carry 30 times its own weight. And a rhinoceros beetle can carry 850 times its own weight. That is like a person carrying two trucks!

◄ A woman with three large pumpkins for Halloween. Some people compete to grow the biggest pumpkins.

COMPARING WEIGHT, MASS, AND VOLUME

YOU WILL NEED

- **Weighing scales**
- **Modeling clay**
- **Small solid rubber ball**
- **Empty shoebox**
- **Large book or some small ones**
- **Pencil and paper**

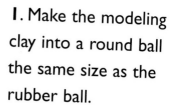

WHAT TO DO

1. Make the modeling clay into a round ball the same size as the rubber ball.

2. Now both balls have the same volume, but do they have the same weight? Weigh the ball of clay on the scales. Then write down how much it weighs.

3. Now weigh the rubber ball. Write down the amount. Is it heavier or lighter than the clay ball?

5. Now weigh a small pile of books or one large book that matches the volume of the shoebox. Write down the amount. Which object weighs the most?

4. Weigh the empty shoebox and write down how much it weighs.

This may help ...

The two balls have the same volume but different weights. The shoebox has the same volume as the books, but it weighs much less. The weight of an object is created by the force of gravity. The more mass something has, the greater the force of gravity. Mass is the amount of matter something is made from. The shoebox is mostly empty space. So, it is made up of less matter than the books—and its mass and weight are less than that of the books.

GLOSSARY

atom A tiny particle. All matter is made up of atoms.

balance A weighing device, often with two pans, used with weights.

carat A tiny weight used to weigh precious metals and gems.

density A measure of how much matter something contains.

force A pushing or pulling action.

gas A substance, such as air, that spreads to fill space.

gram A small unit of weight in the metric system.

gravity The force that pulls things toward Earth.

hundredweight A weight equal to 100 pounds.

imperial The common system of measurement in the United States. Pounds, ounces, inches, and feet are imperial units of measurement.

kilogram A measurement of weight in the metric system.

liquid A type of substance, such as water, that can be poured. Liquids take the shape of their container.

mass The amount of matter something contains.

matter Anything that has weight and takes up space. Solids, liquids, and gases are types of matter.

metric A system that measures things in meters and kilograms.

metric ton A large weight equal to 1,000 kilograms.

milligram A tiny weight equal to 1/1,000 of a kilogram.

ounce A small weight in the imperial system.

pound A heavier weight than an ounce. There are 16 ounces in a pound.

scales A weighing device, often with one or two pans, that includes a pointer or screen showing the weight.

solid A type of substance that is neither a liquid nor a gas.

ton An imperial measurement that weighs 2,000 pounds.

troy A tiny weight used for measuring precious metals and gems.

volume The amount of space something takes up.

weighbridge A huge balance used for weighing cars and trucks.

FIND OUT MORE

BOOKS

Lisa Hill, *Gravity.* Chicago, IL: Raintree, 2009.

Susan Meredith, *Why Do Ships Float?* New York: Chelsea Clubhouse, 2010.

Sean Price, *The Story Behind Gravity*. Chicago, IL: Heinemann Library, 2009.

Navin Sullivan, *Weight*. New York: Marshall Cavendish Benchmark, 2007.

WEBSITES

Johnnie's Math Page
Measurement puzzles designed to increase your measuring ability.
http://jmathpage.com/JIMSMeasurementlengthmassvolume.html

Weight conversion chart
Convert weights from imperial to metric and from metric to imperial.
http://www.sciencemadesimple.com/weight_conversion.php

Publisher's note to educators and parents: Our editors have carefully reviewed these websites to ensure that they are suitable for students. Many websites change frequently, however, and we cannot guarantee that a site's future contents will continue to meet our high standards of quality and educational value. Be advised that students should be closely supervised whenever they access the Internet.

Answers to questions
Page 9: A pencil weighs about ½ ounce; a bag of flour weighs about 5 pounds; a boy (aged 10) weighs about 50 pounds; a man weighs about 175 pounds; and a truck weighs from 10 to 50 tons
Page 11: 3 ounces = 3 x 28 grams = 84 grams; 5 pounds = 5 x 454 grams = 2,270 grams; 6 grams = 6 x 0.04 ounce = 0.24 ounce; 10 kilograms = 10 x 2.2 pounds = 22 pounds
Page 13: There are 60 quarters and 20 nickels
Page 24: The earthworm is 140 grams; the dog is 80 pounds; the adult human is 72 kilograms; the panda is 300 pounds

INDEX